Living in Terror in the World of ISIS:

Living on Pins and Needles

By Sue Ellen

Table of Contents

Introduction..5

Chapter 1: An insight into the formation of ISIS organization...7

Chapter 2: What made possible the formation of the group? 20

Chapter 3: The leader of the Islamic State 26

Chapter 4: What are the techniques used by ISIL fighters? From where did they get their weapons? 33

Chapter 5: Tactics used by ISIS 38

Chapter 6: Why does ISIS continue to dominate? 41

Chapter 7: Does ISIS follow real Islam? 46

Chapter 8: The spiritual beliefs of ISIS members 53

Chapter 9: The Islamic Background of ISIS......59

Chapter 10: Why do Muslims from the West choose to join ISIS? 68

Chapter 11: The ISIS wives.................................75

Chapter 12: Life in a territory dominated by ISIS 81

Conclusion 86

Introduction

In the last years, it is more and more common to hear about the atrocities committed in the name of religion. While some parts of the world continue to develop and become more tolerant; many countries are giving up civilization and starting their journey towards a bloody, unjust war. It is no secret that terrorist groups are perhaps the biggest threat to our security today; and incidences that used to be rare on the news are now part of our daily reality.

In the West, the impact of terrorist groups is becoming more and more striking. While some people blame different ethnic groups or religions; much of the population does not know more than what is presented on the news. The politics and social factors of the Middle East are unfamiliar to many, and it is easy to be deceived by some of the extremist perspectives portrayed in the media.

Let's face the reality: violence has no excuse. There is no acceptable reason for violence of any kind. However, these groups have somehow found or created reasons to kill, scare people, and reign terror upon whole countries. Between abusive regimes and unstable religious leaders; these terror groups have found the perfect climate to develop a cell that would become the main subject of the news in the next months.

This book is meant to explain the formation, motivation, and true intentions standing behind the most bloody and violent terrorist group in the last decade: ISIS.

Chapter 1: An insight into the formation of ISIS organization

What is ISIS, how are they defining themselves, and when did they start to be in the public attention?

«ISIS» is without a doubt, one of the most unpleasant surprises the world has seen in the last few years. They are an armed fundamentalist group and organization that believes in violent change, and a regime dominated by terror and force. With hidden intentions and powerful weapons, they are seeking to gain control over large parts of the Middle East and beyond.

They had previously distanced themselves from any media appearance or social presence, and they were widely unheard of in the West until last year. The terms of membership usually require an intellectual and secure investigation through networking technique, making it almost impossible for the infiltration of army spies. They are choosing their members based on direct affiliation, or careful selection through the Internet, and according to their own criteria. They are considered to be one of the few terrorist groups with a perfect hierarchical structure, and boast a miniscule risk for any information leaks. They were capable of building plans and collecting weapons for years before acting; this alone is perfect proof of how efficient and well-prepared ISIS has become.

The name ISIS is an acronym for "Islamic State in Iraq and Syria." The name was not chosen by the group, nor was it ever officially announced. It is considered to be a strategic move meant to symbolize the unification of all small groups in the area.

The appearance of the "Islamic State in Iraq and the Levant" (ISIL) for the first time was in April of 2013, and it was presented as a result of the unification between the regulatory "Islamic State of Iraq," an organization which belongs to the famous, "Al-Qaeda," and the Syrian organization "Al-Nusra Front." However, the Syrian organization refused the fusion immediately and made a public declaration which denied any connection to the Iraqi organization. This erupted soon enough into a conflict between the two sides in January of 2014, which still remains today.

Another reason for violence, was the ISIS leaders objected publicly to the authority of the "Al Qaeda" leader, Ayman al-Zawahiri, and refused to respond to his call to focus on Iraq, and leave Syria for the Al-Nusra Front. This caused apparent animosity between the two terrorist groups. So began an internal battle for power.

In the beginning, ISIS acted in Iraq under the name, "Tawhid and Jihad group," and later turned to the name, "Al Qaeda in Mesopotamia," after Abu Musab al-Zarqawi inaugurated his leadership in 2004. He openly admitted his support for the Al-Qaeda group, and worked to form an alliance with its former leader, Osama bin Laden. Even if these facts were relatively known by western agencies, the ISIS group did not represent a threat of any kind. If anything, they were considered a small, unarmed group that had no chance of becoming a power in the region.

After Zarqawi was killed in Iraq in June of 2006 by US forces, Abe Hamza al-Muhajir was elected as the new leader. However, a few months later, the formation of "Islamic State of Iraq" was announced under the leadership of Abu Omar Al-Baghdadi. Soon after, he and his assistant, Abi Hamza, were killed by US forces, and the leaders of the organization had the mission, once again, to choose a new successor. Abu Bakr Al-Baghdadi became the new leader of the Islamic State; and with his leadership, a new, violent era started in the history of the group.

Between 2006 and 2010, US and Iraqi forces managed to dramatically weaken the power of the ISIS organization. The Iraqi "Awakening" forces, formed from fighters belonging to Sunni tribes, killed and captured 34 of the top leaders of the Islamic state of Iraq.

After US troops left Iraq in 2011, the bloody revenge of the Islamic state started. In a short time, they managed to launch series of violent bombings in the most important cities of Iraq. The capital, Baghdad, was severely damaged, leaving behind thousands of victims. During subsequent peaceful months, ISIS made great efforts to build a complete arsenal, which they planned to use against the Iraqi army.

From that moment on, chaos surrounding ISIS and its crusade became a political conflict, gradually gaining international attention from the west. Soon after the withdrawal of US forces, few imagined the country would be controlled by terror again. USA offered a reward of 10 million dollars for anyone who would capture or murder the leader, Abu-Bakr Al-Baghdadi. The retaliation of the organization, however, proved exactly how far they were willing to go. They initiated a campaign called "Breaking the walls," which consisted in dozens of attacks on Iraqi prisons. They released hundreds of prisoners who had been jailed by the regime, with a focus on the famous prisons, Abu Ghraib, and Taji, where Sunni Muslims were being held. This was one of the biggest hits for the Iraqi regime, which spurred an introduction to extreme security measures in all facilities.

In April of 2013, Abu Bakr al-Baghdadi said in an audio recording that "Al-Nusra Front ", the Syrian organization, is an extension of the Islamic State organization, and he announced the unification of the two groups under the name of "the Islamic State of Iraq and Syria." However, the Al-Nusra Front leaders were firm in their refusal, and they completely rejected any association with the group.

Abu Bakr took this as a direct attack, and he decided to transfer the activity of the Islamic State in Syria. ISIS soon dominated the Raqqa region, located on the north bank of the Euphrates River, and Deir Al-Zour, which is the seventh largest city in Syria. Soon enough, he installed a regime of terror and took revenge on his disputants by beheading them in public, in the same way his predecessor Zarqawi did.

On June 10, 2014, after the Iraqi forces left, ISIS launched a surprise attack that lead to the control of the city of Mosul, the second biggest city in Iraq after the capital. This offered a new and incredibly useful strategic position for ISIS, and allowed for an ease of control for the larger parts of the region. They expanded their domination to the Saladin province, which connects central Iraq with the north. The city or Baiji, hosting the biggest oil refineries in Iraq, also became part of their newly formed state.

From there they entered in conflict with the armed forces of Kurdistan, where they tried to occupy the city of Kirkuk. The abundance of oil from this city made it an important piece of ISIS's collection. However, the Peshmerga Kurdish forces were fast to occupy the city after the Iraqi army left. Even today there is still a constant battle between the Kurdish forces and ISIS for the control of Kirkuk.

Fast forward a few months, and ISIS was controlling large areas of Iraq, including a big part of the Sunni Al Anbar province, which is the largest province of Iraq. They had already taken under their possession many weapon factories, and were therefore capable of producing their own weaponry supply. On June 29, 2014, they announced publicly the inauguration of the "Islamic Caliphate State," under the leadership of Abu Bakr. The organization would later become infamous under the name of "Islamic State," and its aim was to create a home for all Muslims.

The announcement made by ISIS also required the cancelation of the borders between Iraq and Syria. Also, they required that all Muslims, from all over the world, should migrate to the Islamic state and help with the installation of a new Islamic Country. That was the moment when hundreds of Muslims from all over the world, most especially from the west, decided to leave their country and join ISIS. To this day, there is a continuous and urgent attempt to stop extremist Muslims from joining the terrorist group.

A few days later the organization distributed a video of a speech by Baghdadi. In this first public appearance at the Grand Mosque in the city of Mosul, he called on Muslims to obey his leadership and command. He used religious rhetoric and arguments to engage and attract as many Muslims as possible to his new state. He also appeared in the video with a long grey beard, as well as a black turban and mantle, as this was the traditional clothing of Muslims in the area. The video provoked outrage in Muslim countries where Islamic scholars quickly began to express their disagreement against Abu-Bakr.

After the organization announced the installation of the Caliphate state, the persecution against Christians in the areas of Mosul and Baghdad became one of their main instruments of terror. They targeted all cities with Christian populations, forcing them to leave their homes, or face execution. In many locations, crimes were reported and word of great persecution spread. Soon enough the entire Christian population in the area became desperate to escape from Iraq. The Kurdish areas from northern Iraq were also affected by the persecution, and they began to make public announcements informing Christians to leave the land or face terrifying consequences. Within long, ISIS was capturing former officers from the Iraqi army as an act of revenge for the actions committed against them a few years before. After a series of murders were reported, the Baath Party in Iraq began to lead campaigns against the Islamic State, and the clashes between the two organizations left behind a horrific number of dead civilians. There was no escaping the ghastly reality that had become of the region; whoever tried to oppose ISIS in the areas dominated by them was outnumbered immediately and forced to obey the new regime.

After such a large geographical expansion of the organization, ISIS began looking to improvise new ways to support themselves financially. The reserves of crude oil were big enough to finance the group, so they started to sell oil at a very low price to international and local buyers. Since they controlled large refineries and oil fields in Syria and Iraq under their occupation, their finances grew rapidly, and soon they no longer needed to commit robberies in order to fund their actions.

ISIS could even afford to pay salaries to the fighters, and they were importing goods for the areas that they already had occupied. Not long after, they had sufficient materials to manufacture their own weapons, and they flipped old factories into operational facilities for these purposes. Since they were controlling expansive and important parts of Iraq and Syria, they started to impose fees on the vehicles that were transporting goods through the areas of their control. The civilian transport vehicles could not avoid many of the cities that were under their reign, so the government had no other choice than to pay fees, which would permit them to bring goods into the populated areas. This was one of the things that allowed ISIS to control such a large domain. By limiting the import of goods for the cities under their occupation, they were forcing the government to accept their demands in order to keep the population safe. In many areas they had the power to control the electricity, and they were forcing the authorities to fulfill their requests by threatening power supply. If the local authorities would make any attempt to attack ISIS, they would cut the electricity without further ado.

As we can see, the techniques used by the group are by far not as primitive as those used by Al-Qaeda. By the time they reached the point where they could fund themselves, they could afford to pay salaries for the fighters, and were capable of creating their own weapons. In the clashes with the Iraqi army, ISIS captured as many vehicles as they could, and they became extremely mobile and well armed. Yet another difference found in comparison to the Al-Qaeda group: ISIS could operate in the public space, forcing the government to accept their demands, and slowly gaining the sympathy of Muslim civilians.

Chapter 2: What made possible the formation of the group?

There are a great number of factors that lead to the existence of a favorable environment for the formation of the ISIS terrorist group. Even if we are talking from a political, social or religious point of view; the appearance of a radical Islamic organization was triggered by a certain factor, but still it cannot be motivated or excused. Throughout their takeover, the members of ISIS used many arguments to justify their actions, most of them religious or political. Their intentions are beyond anything honorable, so any motivation exerted is just an attempt to explain an act that is, in essence, unforgivable. The Middle East is already an unstable region where violent clashes are frequent; and in a political and religious background of such instability, the formation of terrorist extremist groups can unfortunately be expected. Any country that tries to impose a severe regime ends up destroyed from the inside by the political rebels. In a world where democracy is a strange ideology, the appearance of these groups is as expected as it is unwanted.

One of the primary reasons for the formation of ISIS is the weakness of the government, the corruption that surrounded the political world, and the decline of Arab nationalism. Also, the presence of a very aggressive and extreme form of Islam created the perfect climate for the appearance of extremist groups.

The Iranian Islamic revolution changed the rules of the society and put the country in a very unstable position. The rise of political Islam in 1979, or the Islamic Revolution in Iran, was a strong attack on the Arabian regimes that were trying to eliminate the religious extremism, and build their societies upon a tolerant foundation. This worked to fill the gap, which resulted from the decline in Arab nationalism, as Iran worked to exert the new ideology that ruled the society. Iran succeeded in this venture, and they strongly supported the Hezbollah party, which was established in Lebanon from the beginning of the 1980's. The Hezbollah party is an armed group with extremist religious foundations, which is also strictly imposing the Shia ideology. The partnership between Iran and the Hezbollah party created outrage in international circles due to the extreme approach being utilized, and the severity of the laws imposed by them.

Another factor that made possible the installation of the Islamic State was the initial attitude of the Arab nations. Not only did the majority of Arab countries refuse to interfere; many of them also saw the Islamic state as the solution for the problems resulting from Sunni Muslims in Iraq and Iran. Egypt, the country with the greatest possibility to interfere, due to its strategic position, was already involved with internal problems of its own. While the Islamic State was rising, Egypt was trying hard to maintain a balanced climate within its own border, as people started to unite against the regime. When Egyptians forced president

Mubarak to step down, the country entered into a very sensitive transitional period, where any political change could trigger another revolution. An intervention against ISIS was impossible during this time, especially because Golf Countries refused to interfere in any way as well.

The economic situation in the Middle East was never great, but in the last years it became tragic for most of the countries. The job market plummeted in just a few months, and overall conditions worsened in the region after the start of the Arab Spring in late December of 2010.

In countries like Syria or Iraq, it became almost impossible for young men to find a job. In a society that forces the man to support the family, this only led to the frustration of the young population. Among the available sources of income, the most attractive and accessible one was found by joining the ISIS organization. Not only were they paying salary to their members, but they were also offering support to their families, and offering them a home. It is easy to see how simple it became for ISIS to convince desperate people to join the group and fight.

In countries like Yemen or Syria, the majority of men were gaining less than 3 $ per day, and that is only if they were able to find a job. Since the governments of Syria and Iraq increased the prices in a desperate attempt to slow down the expansion of ISIS, this minimal income became insufficient for daily needs. Hundreds of desperate men were joining ISIS not necessarily to help build the new Islamic country, but out of necessity to maintain their families, and gain the rights that the regime had taken from them. For the religious extremists, joining in a Holy War was a guarantee that they would reach a promised Paradise. This was alone was reason enough for men to join the terrorist group.

In the areas ruled by Shia extremists, human rights were applicable only for Shia Muslims, while Sunni Muslims were continuously persecuted. ISIS instilled a very intelligent propaganda by publishing recordings of Sunni persecution by Shia extremists. In a region that is constantly in the middle of religious disputes, this was a solid reason for many people to fight against "non-Muslims," as ISIS calls Shia. The hate against Shia expanded to the level where any other religion was not tolerated, and anyone who was found to not be Sunni Muslim was either forced to convert or mercilessly killed.

The religious aspects were and still are the main motivation that Islamic State requires to excuse their inexcusable actions. Even if they are counting on a different, extreme interpretation of the Quran, they identify themselves as Sunni Muslims. Their actions, however, are contradicting many of the principles of Islam. Even if the Middle East consists of a mostly Muslim population, a big part from it is not educated religiously to the level where they actually know the rulings in the Quran. In countries where there is no political or economic stability, religion can quickly become a perfect tool for manipulation.

Chapter 3: The leader of the Islamic State

The ISIS organization developed continuously since Abu Bakr Baghdadi took the lead. Considered to be one of the most dangerous criminal minds in the Middle East; he is the one who first put together the plan of creating an Islamic State. Of course, various religious leaders attempted this before, but none of them had the resources and the criminal intelligence of Abu Bakr. A charismatic and mesmerizing leader, often he appears in public giving speeches about the religious and moral duties of Muslims to encourage Muslims to join the cause and fight for the Islamic State.

The real name of Abu-Bakr Al Baghdadi is Ibrahim Awad Ibrahim Alabdri, but he changed it when he became deeply involved in the terrorist organization. He proclaimed himself as the Caliph Abu Bakr, the second Caliph or prince in Islam after Prophet Mohammed, ruling over the Islamic State and over the Iraqi capital,

Baghdad. His origins are in the city of Samarra, which is located on the east bank of the Tigris River.

He had a normal childhood, and he spent his young years studying In the Islamic University of Baghdad. He acquired a master degree in Quran studies, then he applied for a PhD. He tried to join the Iraqi army, but he was rejected due to an eye defect. Some people say that this was the initial reason why he started to hate the Iraqi government.

Before the American Invasion in 2003, he did not participate in any military action. However, after this he joined Al-Qaeda under the leadership of Osama Bin Laden, and he was influenced by Bin Laden's the extremist perspective. He developed an extraordinary hatred against the western society, and he trained himself to defend the Sunni Muslims from non-believers. Soon after he joined al Qaeda, he became a target for the international agencies, and he even spent time in American prisons. He was known as a fierce fighter without mercy, and with strong religious ideals.

Abu-Bakr was, for a long time, the right hand of Osama Bin Laden. After his death, he became responsible for most of the military activities of Al-Qaeda in Iraq. It was later revealed that Abu-Bakr was responsible for what Al-Qaeda called "the Islam court," which meant that the organization kidnapped people or families based on the accusations of other supporters of the terrorist group. Consequently, the organization then exposed them to a religious court, which often ruled in favor of the death penalty.

The American forces announced the killing of Abu-Bakr, after an air strike they conducted on the borders of Iraq and Syria. It was believed he was dead until the assumption proved to false, when Abu-Bakr accepted the leadership of the Islamic State in 2010. That same year, in the name of revenge, he organized approximately 60 bombings in Baghdad, which created hundreds of victims, and marked the beginning of the expansion of ISIS.

When Abu-Bakr took the leadership of the Islamic State in 2010, the condition of the organization was very unstable. A large number of operations conducted by the American and Iraqi forces against ISIS were successful, and the group lost a large portion of its members during this time. However, Abu-Bakr was able to convince a large number of local fighters to join the terrorist group, and he started his campaign to extend towards the Syrian borders. The 2011 conflict, which had begun in Syria, was the perfect opportunity for ISIS to occupy the cities close to the borders of Iraq, and begin a further expansion of the state.

The leader of Al-Qaeda, Ayman Al-Zawahiri, advised Abu-Bakr repeatedly to not get involved in the Syrian war; but despite his warnings, the dream of Abu-Bakr was to extend the ISIS operations in the north and east of Syria. He would successfully continue to do so in late 2012 and 2013.

Soon after, he occupied large scathes of Iraq and Syria; and from this, ISIS troops evolved from a few isolated cells, into hundreds of fiercely armed groups. He now had control of the borders with Turkey and Jordan, and this made possible the migration of European Muslims towards the Islamic state.

Abu-Bakr stayed far from the lens of the camera and without many public appearances until June of 2014, when the organization distributed footage of Abu-Bakr addressing the entire Muslim word and asking for their obedience. In this same video, he proclaimed himself as the leader of the new created Islamic Caliphate after the prophet Muhammad. He called upon any and all jihadist Muslims in the world to join him and his army, and to help create and strengthen their powerful Islamic Caliphate.

Abu-Bakr is extremely discreet when it comes to public appearances, and he has even avoided the publishing of his voice records. Twenty-four ISIS officers constantly surround him, and the majority of these are middle-aged, Iraqi men who spent time with him in Bucca prison. Also, large portions of these men were officers in Saddam Hussein's army, and they are specialized in military tactics. This specialism allows the fighters to build upon their activity on military plans, unlike Al Qaeda, which demonstrated rather rudimentary methods in contrast.

Abu-Bakr is credited with establishing the entire ideology of the Islamic State, and he took most of his interpretations from Osama Bin-Laden. He was educated since a young age among extremists and dedicated Muslims, and he is capable of creating complicated strategies for the expansion of the Islamic state. He is the one held responsible for dictating the extreme propaganda directed towards foreign Muslims, and he is continuously making constant efforts to increase the number of his fighters. Unlike Al-Qaeda, this organization does not hide or live in caves. They control extensive areas of territory with massive resources and the power of fear; and due to this power, it is impossible for external forces to attack them. Besides, the group was organized by Abu-Bakr in such an effective way, that any leakage of information could be detected immediately. The new members of the organization are not informed on the details of the future operations. Rather, they are simply fighters receiving and obeying orders. Only after months of fighting inside the State are they are considered trustworthy members. This system established by Abu-Bakr is the main reason why ISIS has had the success that Al-Qaeda never conquered.

Chapter 4: What are the techniques used by ISIL fighters? From where did they get their weapons?

One of the most intriguing things since the development of ISIS was the massive amount of weapons they have acquired, and the manner in which they obtained their resources, war vehicles, and ammunition in such a short time.

The weapons they have find uses beyond the battlefield, as they are also used to train the recruits in the camps and keep the civilian population in a mindset of fear. Their military operations require a massive funding for the purchase of weapons and ammunition, and for obtaining access to the logistic services and salaries for fighters. If we take the example of the current US military action in Iraq and Syria, the limited military operations against what is called "Islamic State" have cost around $312,000 per hour, according to the American agencies. We can only imagine that the Islamic State needs at least an amount equal to this in order to face the offensive, and continue to expand and control the territory. They are unlike any other terrorist organization with the utilization of the Internet for their viral propaganda; and they are funding a few other terrorist cells throughout different parts of the Middle East as well.

Despite the high cost of buying weapons and the difficulty in obtaining them; Syria has become a vital and important center for the trade and smuggling of weapons of various kinds, even after three years after the start of the Civil War. Unfortunately the country experiences a severe lack of resources, with the exception of deadly weapons.

The method utilized by the ISIS organization to retrieve the newest weapons and equipment is still controversial among both local and international circles. Some sources indicate that the intelligence agencies of several countries are providing weapons, while other sources confirm that ISIS receives weapons from Arms traffickers. However, an amount of their guns and equipment is produced in the factories under their control throughout Syria and Iraq. Places that were previously used to manufacture metal objects or clothes are now used for the arsenal of the troops.

There are some alleged sources for weapons retrieved by ISIS, but none of them can be confirmed as the group strictly prevents the leakage of any and all information. One of the possible sources of their ammunition appears to be Sudan, a country where conflicts have completely trampled any remaining peace. After the Iraqi army analyzed the ammunition of ISIS, they discovered it is the same type produced and used in Sudan. The organization has no difficulty paying large amounts of money for their supplies, and Sudan is on the brink of an economic crisis, where a large part of the population is searching for alternative sources of money.

ISIS controls expansive reserves of oil and petrol fields, and they are a gold mine for weapon smugglers of the Middle East. The region is already known for the extensive black market from which it is possible to purchase anything from weapons to bombs and military vehicles.

Since the beginning of the conflicts, ISIS has seized a heavy amount of weapons from not just the Iraqi army, but also the Syrian military forces. The regime of Bashar al-Assad has been the main source of weapons for Russia, and after the conflicts there is a potential to observe the presence of a large number of Russian weapons in the hands of the terrorist group.

Saudi Arabia, Qatar and the United Arab Emirates and Jordan have all supported the Syrian opposition groups through providing them with large quantities of military equipment. The delivery of those weapons is both complex and unclear at this time.

The intelligence agencies declared that the terrorist group has a large supply of weapons from the Al-Qaeda cell, and from the armed rebels in Syria and Iraq. During the conflicts with the Kurds, the organization took all the weapons, materials, and ammunition they could find, leaving the Kurdish army in a great shortage of weapons. This shortage was later solved upon receiving external supplies.

Chapter 5: Tactics used by ISIS

One of the reasons that allowed ISIS to expand so quickly and gain control on such a large territory is their image portrayed in mainstream media. In the beginning, they were seen in a similar light to other known terrorist groups: poorly armed, counting on a small number of troops, and without the capacity to fight against a real army. However, the terrorist group proved to demonstrate a very effective intellectual infrastructure. They are building their plans using military strategy, and they are not, by any means, using the same rudimentary techniques utilized by Al-Qaeda.

When the Al-Qaeda appeared in Iraq under the leadership of Abu Musab al-Zarqawi in 2004; it was shown having occupied villages and neighborhoods in some cities and towns of Anbar, where it was a powerful resentment against the Iraqi government as well as American troops. This enabled the Al-Qaeda for the first time since its inception to work publicly within towns and villages. Still, the organization was constantly performing operations such as those operate with suicide car bombs or explosive belts.

In Syria, the tactics have since changed. The State of Islam in Iraq and Syria (ISIS) became independent from Al-Qaeda because of the large disagreement between Abu Bakr al-Baghdadi, "Leader of ISIS," and Ayman al-Zawahiri, "Leader of Al-Qaeda." This dispute was finally ended through the declaration of an Islamic caliphate. ISIS started to form a real army consisting of thousands of fighters, and an international mobilization system which brings fighters from North Africa, the Gulf countries, southern Russia, Central Asia, and Europe, to Syria and Iraq, through Turkey.

ISIS was able to occupy vast lands in Al-Raqqah, Alanbar, and Nineveh, by adopting a distinctive tactical plan employing many major strategic components. First, they left no clues for what their next target would be, always keeping the element of surprise in their back pocket. Nobody expected the attacks over Raqqa and Mosul in Iraq. Not only this, but they are completing attacks in open areas, without trying to use hidden roads like Al-Qaeda used to do.

Furthermore, they are using a large number of armed forces against targets that have no means of self-defense. ISIS needed only one week to occupy over one hundred villages in the countryside of the Syrian city, Kobani. When necessary, they depend on suicide bombers who are exploding their way into buildings or cities. They are consistently using the "shock and awe" factor through fast, bloody attacks, and the release of viral images revealing the massacres. Via the Internet, they have released several videos of their beheadings and mass executions, which are meant to spread terror and discourage any attempt at retaliation from the locals.

Chapter 6: Why does ISIS continue to dominate?

There are many reasons that allowed ISIS to achieve success in battles throughout Iraq, Syria and Libya. These reasons are both internal and external.

The internal reasons that helped ISIS to dominate big areas in Arabian countries are mainly related to the political situation and the economic crisis.

In the countries fighting an oppressive regime, the internal agencies are supporting ISIS with their fight against the government. This is because the brutality of ISIS is, very often, directed towards the same regime that exploited the population for many years. Civilians in many areas are supporting ISIS with hopes they will get rid of the corrupted government, and instead bring up a strong country ruled by Islamic law. However, ISIS is often killing these same civilians, who face the difficult decision of staying under their reign, or leaving with the terror of a horrific punishment for the violation of ISIS regulations.

ISIS has received tremendous support from Sunni tribes in Iraq. They provided the terror group with all possible means, from money to weapons, in order to help them achieve their plans and free the Sunni population from the control of Shia militants.

The outrage in Syria against the current Bashar Alassad regime helped ISIS in finding a supreme environment to start their operations in Syria. They consider themselves part of the Syrian revolution, when in fact they are only oppressing instead of helping the Syrian population. Every day, thousands of Syrians are trying to escape the conflict zone, in an attempt to reach the European coast on illegal ships. European countries have offered asylum to a big number of Syrian refugees, and they expect more to arrive within the proceeding months.

The strong media system of ISIS is one of the most important weapons of this terrorist group. They are actively using all possible media outlets such as Radio, TV, and all major social networks to broadcast footage supporting their victories. They have a successful propaganda system, and they have media specialists building up their public image. They are trying to show themselves as a shield against the non-Islamic population the occupied Iraq or Syria. Unsurprisingly, their propaganda has attracted extremists from all over the world, who fled to Syria with hopes to join the fight against oppressors. Also, they have a strong network constantly boosting materials to present ISIS as a very powerful group. They are creating footage that shows their training routines and the efficiency of their soldiers; and they are creating a horrific image that instills fear and strongly discourages any attempt at retaliation.

A strategic move by ISIS was to take advantage of the religious aspects that they are preaching.

They are recruiting new members who share the same extremist ideology, and they educate them to believe the fight against non-Muslims is an honorable sign of faith. Confessions from people who escaped ISIS camps reveal how they hold classes daily, ensuring their fighters are fully dedicated to the religious purpose. ISIS is able to monitor these classes and consequently select for battle those members who are most ready to sacrifice themselves in the name of religion.

The fact that they are controlling some of the largest petroleum reserves in the area ensures a massive budget allowance for the group. They have an income of almost two million dollars a week from oil exports, and they can easily afford to buy the latest technology off the black market. A recent video revealed how one member purchased a new smart phone that had just been released on the market. The other terrorist cells, such as Al-Qaeda, were forced to live in caves, and without modern facilities, while ISIS has an easy reach to the latest technological devices.

They can also afford to give big salaries to their fighters, which is a powerful motivation in an area where extreme poverty is rampant.

For a long time, the Arab nations, Europe, and USA ignored the activity in the area because ISIS did not present a serious threat. In the beginning, the group was relatively small and located in just a minute area of Iraq. In a matter of months they expanded into a large part of the Middle East, and have unified all terrorist cells in Syria. Now, there are around 1,000 groups fighting together to create the new Islamic State, and this makes any attack on the ground nearly impossible.

Chapter 7: Does ISIS follow real Islam?

There are many contractions surrounding this question, and while the world presents them as Muslim extremists, many of their actions contradict even the strictest interpretations of Islam. If, in the beginning, there was an understanding of their actions from a civilian point of view; their bloody and violent actions in the last year would have changed the perception of the public to identify them as terrorists. The most important Islamic scientists agree that their methods and motivations are not Islamic; and in a desperate attempt they released an official letter to ISIS, using religious rhetoric and arguments to ask them to stop the fighting. The letter consisted of various Islamic laws that were broken by ISIS and warnings about the divine punishment the terror group would receive. Sure enough, ISIS did not respond to this, and they did not do anything to stop the violent domination.

The actions of ISIS are contradicting Islam on many points, and some of the most shocking examples are found in their recent actions, which have stirred an outrage throughout the entire world.

The burning of the Jordanian pilot Muath al-Kasasbeh was showed in a video released by the terror groups a few months back. This is considered one of the cruelest acts of violence committed by ISIS in the last year. However, a fact that is known and accepted by Muslim scientists is that setting any creature, animal, or human afire, under any circumstance, is strictly forbidden by Islam, and it can not be justified with any kind of religious argument. The method is not to be used for either torture or execution, and even the incineration of bodies after death is unacceptable. This was one of the biggest proofs to the public that ISIS is not following the Islamic rulings, and therefore they cannot be considered Muslims.

On top of this, there have appeared many pictures on the Internet wherein members of the group appear to be praying. All Muslims in the world pray facing one single direction, Mecca, which is the religious center of Islamic religion. In contradiction to this, the ISIS members were shown praying in another direction, which is considered invalid in Islam.

Yet another point that has attracted public disapproval was that it is prohibited in Islam to declare people non-Muslims until they declare themselves. Yet ISIS is calling any disputant non-Muslim as a justification for their actions. Even if most of their victims are Sunni Muslims, they are using their own arguments to declare them as non-believers and to have an excuse for murder. They have applied this principle against many civilians in Iraq and Syria, and they ended up killing hundreds of Muslim men, women and children. Islam has very strict rules for war, and the killing of women and children is forbidden unless it is out of self-defense.

It is well known that ISIS caused massive destruction in the city of Mosul where they captured, tortured and killed a great number of women, both Muslim and non-Muslim. There are many testimonials from women held as slaves in ISIS camps, of how only a few of them survived. However, slavery was a practice prohibited by the Islam world hundreds of years ago, and the religious leaders of the world have agreed that this is not a religious practice, but rather a barbaric one that contradicts any religious, moral or human law.

Recently, ISIS published a video showing the killing of 21 Egyptian Christians who were working in Libya as constructors. In Islam there are specific rules forbidding the harming or killing of any person who does not attack you, especially the people of the scripture: Christians and Jews. Christians exist in big communities in Islamic countries and they live in peace, protected by the laws of Islam, which encourage Muslims to treat them as any other human being. Despite this, ISIS continues to follow their own rules, finding excuses for the executions of innocent people.

The opinions of several Islamic leaders and scientists are very clear regarding the matter, and all of them disapprove the actions of the terrorist group.

Al-Azhar is the biggest Islamic institution in the world, as well as Sunni Islam's most prestigious center of learning. The grand Imam of Al-Azhar, Ahmed Al Tayb, declared publicly that ISIS actions are not from Islam, and that the deeds of ISIS require the punishment which is mentioned in the Quran for all those oppressors who fight against the words of God and his prophet. He made an appeal to all Muslims throughout the world to not join ISIS for the illusion of a holy war. He also added, "Islam forbids killing of the innocent human soul... It forbids mutilating the human soul by burning or in any other way even during wars against an enemy that attacks you."

Even though the Kingdom of Saudi Arabia follows one of the strictest forms of Islam, The Saudi Grand Mufti Sheikh, Abdul Aziz al-Sheikh, has announced that ISIS is, "enemy number one," of Islam. He added that: "All the methods of these groups are false. There are things behind them and there is no good in them. We do not trust them or trust their people. Whoever invites our youth to join these misguided factions is mistaken and is straying far away from the right path."

Despite the different interpretation they gave to the Quran, the most important Islamic institutions, have declared ISIS the primary enemy of Islam, and they firmly exert religious arguments to support this decision. Frankly, ISIS had a terribly indirect impact over Muslims that live in non-Islamic countries, as the populations of these countries directed some anger towards them. Attacks and insults from the public upon those considered to be supporters of ISIS are increasingly frequent. The truth, this organization has other motivations behind their actions that are more political than religious. Since the actions of the group are directed towards political institutions, and they are using the Muslim population as a weapon, it's easy to see why the entire Islamic World is trying to fight against them.

Chapter 8: The spiritual beliefs of ISIS members

Even if the intentions behind the ISIS actions are not pure, some of the group's fighters truly believe that this is the right path towards divine paradise, and they are counting on religious aspects for this reason.

ISIS' interpretation of Islam is the strictest form, which means they try to apply what they consider to be pure Islam. This means the laws imposed by the Islamic State are the same as those followed in the time of the Prophet Mohammed. No addition or modern variation of Islam is accepted.

According to their beliefs, whoever will fight against non-believers will be rewarded in the Paradise, and if they die in the battle, they will become martyrs. This is why many religious Muslims do not hesitate to launch themselves into a suicidal mission against non-believers; they believe this will offer them the supreme reward for a Muslim: Paradise. It is considered the holy duty of any practicing Muslim to fight in the holy wars, and to sacrifice themselves for God. Many ISIS fighters are educating their children to be ready at any time to leave their life and follow the path of war.

ISIS fighters very often use the term "Jihad" as replacement for war. Jihad is an Islamic term, which translates as "battle." Nowadays, it is often confused with "holy-war," but the true interpretation describes the term, Jihad, as the struggle that each person will face in his lifetime. For example, the struggle a young Muslim will have to not drink alcohol is considered his personal Jihad; therefore the term has nothing to do with what is described by mainstream media. However, extremist scholars attribute the meaning of "holy-war" to this term, which means religious war. Since ISIS was originally fighting against Shia, they consider this battle as one necessary to defend their religion and other Muslims against non-believers.

As a matter of fact, the expansion of the Islamic state accelerated when the abuse of Sunni Muslims by Shia became very severe, and the corrupted regimes did nothing to protect the population. All pure intentions were lost along the way, along with the original founders of the group. Similarly, the main trigger of the fights in Syria was the oppressive Shia regime, which kept the Sunni population in a state of terror.

Furthermore, the Islamic State is applying the Sharia law, or, the original Islamic Law. The only country in the world that still applies this is Saudi Arabia, but they have accepted a revised version of it, and are even considering some more modern revisions. However, the Islamic state is applying the exact punishments used in the times of the Prophet. These punishments are not Islamic, and the majority of them are not even mentioned in the Quran. They are adapting the religious rules to their own criteria, thinking it is their duty to apply the law of God.

Extremist Muslims have desired the installation of an Islamic State for hundreds of years. Leaders of ISIS do not even consider Saudi Arabia religious, although they are considered the strictest Islamic country in the world. ISIS has threatened to attack the kingdom a number of times, vowing that by accepting modern elements they are damaging the true meaning of Islam. The installation of the Caliphate, however, is not permissible from an Islamic point of view. Islamic scholars declared a number of times that it is strictly prohibited to create an Islamic state without the collective approval of all Muslim nations. However, Abu-Bakr, the self-proclaimed Khalifa of Muslims believes Muslim nations must obey him, and those who refuse, are not actually Muslims, and therefore deserve severe punishment according to the law of God. When asked why he is conducting attacks against Sunni Muslims, he answered that whoever is not with him as part of the Islamic state, is against him.

As for the women, in normal circumstances it is prohibited to relocate yourself in another country without a mahram, meaning a man of the family. However, any woman who will make this trip with the intention to relocate in a religious community will be rewarded. Hijrah is an Islamic term used for the relocation or migration from the land of unbelievers to the Islamic land. The term's origins stem from the time of the prophet Mohammed. This practice has begun once more, with the hundreds of Muslims who are migrating from Europe to the Islamic State. The women who perform this journey are called Muhajira, and it is considered obligatory to relocate yourself if you are afraid that you will give in to the temptations of the unbelievers, or, "fitnah." It is a very important part of a Muslim woman's life to get married, and religious women believe that by marrying a soldier of God they will go to Paradise with their husband. The role of women in Islamic communities is as important as the man's. They are taking care of the supplies and equipment, and some women supervise dress code on the streets, and almost everything else that does not deal with the fighters' duty of battle.

Chapter 9: The Islamic Background of ISIS

Islamic principles applied by ISIS and how it affects the group's operations.

The Islamic world was the target of discrimination for many years. Even if the holy book of Islam, the Quran, has only one unaltered version, the Arabic language makes its interpretation very difficult. There are many ways to understand the rulings from the Quran and even if most Muslims adopted the moderate version of Islam, there will still be groups of Muslims who think it's necessary to apply the far stricter religious principles.

The Islamic world is actually divided into 2 major branches; the 1st branch is Sunni Islam, which represents the majority of Islam and most Muslims around the world. Therefore Sunni Islam does not have a specific demographic pattern. The 2nd branch is Shia Islam, and it is localized in countries like Iran, Iraq, and Azerbaijan, in addition to minority groups in

Lebanon, Syria, Indonesia, and Pakistan. There are some small groups of Shia in other countries of the Middle East; but after the conflict between ISIS and Shia began to elevate, Shia Muslims relocated to areas of the countries where Shia where they would be part of a majority group.

The appearance of ISIS in Iraq was directed mainly against the US army, Shia militias, and the ruling government, which was largely led by Shia Muslims. Moreover, the revolution in Syria was against Bashaar Alassad, also Shia; it is easy to consequently see that ISIS bears a Sunni ideology. The problem is that Sunni ideology has many far more varying principles than Shia. Some of the things considered untouchable in Sunni Islam, such as the Prophet Muhammad, or the perfection of the Quran, were topics of great debate in the Shia world. There is a big discrepancy between Shia and Sunni groups, and for years this brought forth issues of animosity when the groups were brought together.

There are many Sunni Islamic schools and each one holds a different interpretation of the Quran and Sunna. Sunna is both a tradition and way of life of the Prophet Mohammed, the prophet of Islam. Most of interpretations of Sunna are very similar with the exception of a few verses. The differences are due to the Arabic language, which can be understood in many different ways. The main points of Islam are widely agreed upon, and their differences are, for the most part, accepted by all parts as well. The majority of Muslims in the world are following what is called, balanced Islam, which refers to the middle way, avoiding extremes and experiencing all things in moderation. This Islam model dominates in bigger Islamic countries like Indonesia, Egypt, Turkey, Nigeria, and Malaysia. Most Europeans and Americans who choose to convert to Islam are accepting Moderate Islam, which has nothing to do with the violent interpretation applied by ISIS. Unfortunately, the lack of knowledge from the media and the misconceptions put Muslims all over the world in a very unfortunate position. Since the appearance of ISIS, cases of discrimination and attacks on Muslims in the West have become quite common. Islamic communities are trying hard to educate the public and create a safe environment for Muslims to live in peace.

Even if most Muslims are moderate, some Sunni schools are very strict in their application of Islamic teachings, claiming that Muslims must follow the interpretation of Islamic scientists in the first centuries of Islam. These interpretations do not allow variation due to modern life, and in general are highly based on traditions, rather than adequate evidence from the Quran. There are a few places that accept this version of Islam, the biggest being the Kingdom of Saudi Arabia, which is considered one of the strictest and most religious countries. The law of the country is based upon Sharia, the law of Islam, and still applies religious-based punishments for any and all crimes. There is a strong international lobby for the support of women in Saudi Arabia, since women do not have the same rights as men. The most obvious law is that women are forbidden to drive or leave the country without a "mahram," the term for a male member of the family.

Some local communities from Sudan, Nigeria, and a part of Afghanistan, still apply this ideology of extreme Islam. These communities are often disturbed by religious conflicts caused by terrorist groups inside their borders, and the opposition of such terror groups to the emancipation of women.

These strict Islamic schools embrace Wahabism, which is named after Muhammad Ibn Abd Alwahab. He was a preacher and scholar that lived in KSA 300 years ago and his interpretations of the verses of Quran are still strictly kept and followed.

ISIS apparently belongs to the Wahabiya School of "Wahabism" which is the strictest version of Sunni Islam. This explains why ISIS has attracted members from all over the world, as there are adepts of this ideology everywhere, in contrast to the Shia ideals that only thrive in countries like Iran or other local communities.

Bearing Sunni ideology also gave ISIS the opportunity to penetrate every Muslim community throughout the world from east to west, owing to the worldwide distribution of Sunni Islam. Hence, when ISIS occupied Iraqi cities like Mosul, the citizens from this city did not show any resistance to ISIS. Rather, they welcomed the fighters, since the city is one of the major Sunni cities in Iraq, and it existed under the persecution of Shia militants. The government therefore considered ISIS to be the better alternative. This was, perhaps, the greatest advantage ISIS had. Most terrorist groups do not have support from civilians and live in hiding. On the other hand, ISIS was ruling cities and replacing a corrupted government. Even if their ideology was extreme, they provided for the civilians protection and good resources, things that were considered a luxury under the dominance of Shia militants.

Historically there is a frank and an obvious clash between Sunni and Shia Muslims, which ranges from simple student debates in the university, political and parliamentary arenas, and even bloody conflicts. Disputes arose from varying understandings of the religion, as well as the political context in the area, which encouraged the two sides to fight against each other. Some extremists from both sides often led online campaigns against the other, in an attempt to convert and show the opposing group what they think is the correct interpretation of the Quran.

These historic clashes naturally produced many armed organizations on both sides, which seek out violent domination. These organizations interfere in most of the current wars happening in the Middle East. The Hezbollah party in Lebanon, who shared in the war against Israel to recapture the south of Lebanon from the Israeli occupation, currently supports the Syrian regime and Bashar Alassad in Syria. Another armed organization is Liwa Abu al-fadl al-Abbas, meaning, "the Brigade of Abu al-fadl al-Abbas," which is a Shia Iraqi militant group operating in Syria, and working in an attempt to stop the expansion of ISIS.

Another notable armed Shia group is Houthis army, which has operated in and controls Yemen after their COUP in September of 2014. Yemen, which was a relatively peaceful region, recently became involved in the area's religious clashes, and is currently one of the most affected countries in the Middle East.

We must take into consideration another reason for the highly charged atmosphere in the Middle East, and that is the accelerating role and interference of Iran, "The Biggest Shia country," and other Sunni countries like Lebanon, Yemen, and Syria. This interference takes many forms, from the support of the media, for example in the case of the Bahrain demonstration against the ruling Sunni royal family in Bahrain, or military aids to the Houthis army in Yemen. The Hezbollah organization in Lebanon and Syria also commit financial support to the current regime in Syria led by Bashar Al asad.

Chapter 10: Why do Muslims from the West choose to join ISIS?

Since the begging of ISIS, there was a constant and efficient effort to gather Muslims from all over the world to fight against the non-believers and help create the new Islamic State. The surprising fact is that most Muslims who chose to join are not extremists from the Middle East; rather they are educated people from the West, and most of the time were not even born Muslims. There is an alarming tendency among European, converted Muslims to accept the extremist ideas of ISIS and relocate to Syria. The European authorities are trying to stop this process; but it is difficult to control such a large and diverse population, especially because most of them are not registered as Muslims nor present a known threat.

The sophisticated methods employed by ISIS are far from the primitive methods used by Al-Qaeda. While Al-Qaeda only used direct recruitment in some isolated areas; the ISIS organization continues to make public requests towards Muslims from all over the world. For a young mind, the excitement of an adventure is reason enough to initiate dangerous actions without even considering the religious factor.

The ISIS organization has market strategies more effective than many international agencies today. They have gone so far as to publish a magazine in June of 2014, which promoted their actions and was translated in several languages. They distributed the magazine massively, especially on the Internet and on all social media platforms. In a time where social media clogs much of our daily activity, this was an easy and efficient way to contact and spread the ISIS message to young, easy-to-influence Muslims around the world. The terror group designed the magazine to promote their values using religious and moral arguments, and they urged that is the moral duty of any Muslims to take part in the war against non-believers. Soon after, the ISIS organization even created a clothing line promoting their logo, manufacturing the clothing in the Syrian factories under their occupation. In further efforts to claim the minds of the youth, they even created a video game called, "Salil Sawarim." This was the perfect venue for manipulating young attracted to gaming. ISIS has and will continue to exploit all the resources available, to make sure their message is easy to find and understand by any Muslim in the world.

ISIS created an "electronic army" with the mission of making online propaganda and convincing young Muslims to join them. They have a solid grasp on the art of persuasion, and are capable of motivating their actions through invented religious ideologies. They periodically release footage from training camps and the battlefront. By showing their moments of victory, and the manner in which they enforce "true Islam" in areas controlled by Shia; they can make Muslims believe their actions are honest, and that joining them is a moral duty necessary for reaching the everlasting paradise.

The fact that the organization is formed mostly by young people is one its greatest dangers. Al-Qaeda was counting on primitive ways of persuasion; but ISIS has found far more efficient ways to reach the public, and show the image of young, educated men who are risking their lives in the job of God. By having recruits from all countries is also a great achievement; they can translate their documents in any language, and they can discuss and recruit people in their own language. Very often, on the Internet they are not instigating for violence or revenge, but rather they are adopting a humble attitude, showing empathy with the oppressed Muslims, and using different verses of Quran to convince others to fight. They even give clear instructions on how to reach their camps, claiming that the border of Syria is the meeting place. From there, the organization will escort them and begin training. There is an attempt in controlling the traffic from Turkey to Syria, but it is difficult considering the region is enflamed with war.

They are not only using religious arguments; they are actually offering jobs for highly qualified Muslim experts. For example, ISIS created a company for recruiting engineers to work on the petroleum station that they are exploiting. Many poor, educated Muslims from all over the world choose to follow the glimmer of an attractive salary on ISIS rule, rather than lead a life of misery in their own country. Doctors who were supposed to work in camps were also needed in ISIS territories, so the group began campaigns on the Internet offering impossible-to-refuse salaries and, as a bonus, a chance to join the Paradise.

For men who join ISIS, it is considered an obligation to get married. Therefore, in their recruitment campaigns they are offering wives for the single men who choose to join the war, and a home in the areas controlled by them. It is the most effective and extended recruitment campaign in the history, simply because they are offering money, the perspective of marriage, a home, and a religious life.

ISIS is constantly publishing materials showing fighters doing normal activities like playing video games. This is meant to convince the public that the life they live inside of the Islamic State is a normal one, where they can still enjoy modern aspects of life, but without the temptations of non-believers. They are calling the Islamic State a "family" and are inviting new members to join them. Of course, many international agencies try to infiltrate spies into the organization with hopes to obtain information about the plans and strategies of the group. The problem is, the hierarchical system is so efficient and the plans are so well built that for a newcomer it is impossible to have access to anything that could aid external forces. Not only this, but they are controlling the communication with the outside world, and any leakage of information is detected immediately.

They have created the illusion of a "paradise on earth" as some of them describe it; a place with a peaceful existence, where they form strong bonds and lead a religious life away from any sinful temptation. They offer attractive professional perspectives and the possibility of marrying a religious woman. All these together are more than enough to convince hundreds of western Muslims to join them. When the discrimination against Muslims became more intense, they offered a refugee from the non-believers, attracting naive Muslims into their trap of terror.

Chapter 11: The ISIS wives

As expected, not only Muslim men were attracted by the idea of a religious life. Muslim women from all over the world, most of them born and raised in secular countries, left their families behind to join the organization. They are using the same method as men, traveling to the borders of Syria, from where they are taken by fighters and put into special homes for women. The mirage of a successful marriage is very powerful for women, who were raised to believe in the sanctity and obligation of marriage.

The ones who are leading the recruitment campaigns are not men, but mostly women. They are acting on the major social media networks and encouraging young Muslim women to join the ISIS organization and marry a fighter.

They have created blogs and special accounts that describe the life in the camps for the women and how they are dealing with their new status. Most of them are using a humble tone, describing how their new life is very close to God, and how they fulfilled their duty as religious women by joining the religious war. They are posting pictures with their meals, and they share funny stories, together with other wives in their camp. This creates an image of normality, and the illusion of a deep friendship between ISIS wives.

They are even advised to bring certain amenities from their countries, like cosmetics and shoes, because the products they find inside of the camp are not high quality. Also, they are recommended to bring their own Islamic clothes, which are obligatory for all women inside the camp. This type of clothing is also encountered in Saudi Arabia and, sometimes, in other Islamic countries. In the Quran it is recommended for women to cover their hair and wear loose, decent clothing that will not attract the attention of men. However, they are allowed to show their hands and face. and there are no regulations on the color or exact style of the clothes. ISIS, on the other side, applies a more strict interpretation, and they support the idea that women must not show any part of their body except the eyes. Therefore, all women inside ISIS camps wear what is called "niqab," a type of clothing that covers the entire body, leaving just a small space for the eyes and not revealing any shape of the body. They are also wearing gloves, and are completely prohibited from using perfume or any kind of cosmetic outside the home. In the home, in front of their husband, they have no restrictions.

Women who live in the ISIS camps share stories from their daily activities of how they got married. One woman who writes a blog on the Internet under the name, "Mother of the lion," tells how her new life is similar to the life of any housewife in the west. They are spending most of their time cooking, cleaning, or completing Islamic courses. Also, they are recommending for any woman who lost her husband in the battle to get married again as soon as possible, because life in the camp is limited for a single woman. Apparently, single men and women live in separate houses and they have little to no contact with each other, while married couples receive their own house. However, most women do not see their husband more than a few times per month, as they are constantly away in battle.

The members of the organization arrange marriages. When a single woman comes, soon the process of finding a suitable husband begins. Most often, they will get married the first time they see each other, without having the chance to meet or talk before the ceremony.

There have even been several cases of teenagers from Europe, who left their countries to join the battle and marry with fighters. However, after a few weeks they posted messages online where they asked for help returning to their own country. Clearly, the image of a friendly and religious life is not so close to reality. Unfortunately it is almost impossible for the authorities to interfere as long as the women are being held in the camps. There are warnings in all Muslim communities about the ways ISIS members manipulate young women, and the dangers they will face if they chose to go there. Once they have entered the camps, they have no chance of getting out alive. Most of them are pushed into taking Arabic courses, but the most used language in the camp is English as the members come from all over the world.

For religious girls, the idea of reaching Paradise is more appealing than the luxury of a modern life in Europe. According to some interpretations of Islam, whoever takes part in the Jihad, or the holy war, will enter Paradise. This also includes the wives of the fighters. Some women share their disappointment that for now, there is no place for women in the battle because they have too many men already. Even so, some of them are relocating to Syria with hopes to become a part of the battle. Another ISIS wife tells how, whenever her husband has time he will take her outside to practice firing a weapon. With the rest of their time, the women take intensive courses of Arabic and Quran studies. They are also trained on how to make the best Internet propaganda for the recruitment of more women.

The greatest targets are those Muslim women with unhappy family lives or extreme religious views. On Twitter, ISIS has an active presence, and they are tweeting religious sayings meant to convince naive women to join them. Above all, they are warning them of the dangers of living among non-believers in western societies.

Chapter 12: Life in a territory dominated by ISIS

Even if life inside the camps is presented as somehow idyllic for the fighters and their wives, the reality is vastly different. The civilians in the areas controlled by ISIS are constantly trying to escape, and the risk for being killed is certain death. The cities are true battlefields, and ISIS troops do not hesitate to use civilians as human shields in an attack. They are also constantly robbing the cities, taking anything they might need, from animals to vehicles or money.

The Islamic Caliphate is built on very strict ideologies, and whoever does not follow their rules, will be tortured and killed. Most journalists who made their way into the territory controlled by ISIS were decapitated, as the group considers any stranger a direct threat the security of the group. People who escaped from the area are afraid to share details, because most of them still have families living in the area whose lives would be placed in consequent danger.

Those with the courage to talk are telling stories about living in terror, with any move controlled and approved by ISIS. Any element that is not considered compatible with their extremism is eliminated immediately. People can be killed if they have the wrong movie or listen to music. For drinking alcohol the punishment is death, and the same goes for adultery and a plethora of other crimes.

One fighter that escaped from the camps confessed they were forced to take courses of Sharia, Islamic law, and interpretation of Quran; but in these courses they were not teaching the exact verses from the Quran. Instead they taught the meaning they prescribed to it. Basically, they were using the foundation of Islam, and building their own twisted ideology, forcing the fighters to apply their own version of Islam into daily life.

In the villages under their occupation, strict Sharia law is applied. All men must have a beard, and all women must completely cover their face. There are members of the organization who are watching the streets daily, punishing those people who do not follow the strict dress code. For exposing your face as a woman, you can be punished with up to 50 lashes. It is forbidden to talk with men on the street or wear perfume. Since most ISIS soldiers are young people, it is easy to indoctrinate them with their strict rules.

When they are first opening a new city, they use a decisive technique of promising people great things, such as restoring electric lines and ensuring the security that the old regime did not provide. This is motivating many people to join the forces and help them settle their domination. However, as soon as they are installed in the new city, they declare the new regime and punish anyone who dares to oppose them.

In many areas of Syria, the conflict between ISIS and the Syrian regime leads to extreme poverty. Cities that used to be populated are now completely empty. Only the bombed ruins of houses are left behind. The population either escaped from the country, or moved to the cities that are still secure. Due to the war, any import of goods is stopped, and the prices increased almost 10 times since last year. It is nearly impossible now for a family to support themselves. Another problem is the lack of homes. ISIS troops forced families to leave their homes and relocate. What was left was destroyed by the bombings. Now, thousands of people live in improvised shelters and have no chance of leaving the country. Most of the area dominated by ISIS is continuously under attack from outside forces; even if they are allowed to live in their homes, a looming fear remains of the likelihood they will be killed.

In Iraq, they Islamic State is constantly keeping the population in terror with night bombings and shortage of provisions. They are organizing blockades on the most important routes between Syria and Iraq, and they are searching for Christians or Shia. There are several videos released on the internet revealing ISIS troops stopping cars, checking the identity of the passengers, and killing whoever is not Sunni Muslim, or appears to be against them.

In the northern part of Iraq, the ISIS army is constantly fighting against the Kurdish forces. They have devastated the communities, and they have taken women as prisoners. There are confessions of women who were held as sexual slaves for members of ISIS or were forced to convert to Islam and marry a fighter. The only ones who escaped were those with children, or who were too old to get married. Many of them committed suicide, preferring death to a life in captivity. There was an international crisis after ISIS published instructions on the Internet about how to deal with war slaves, and how to sell them. There were even holding markets where they sold Kurdish women. This is one additional proof of the barbarity of ISIS: entire communities in the area are leaving everything behind to flee before ISIS reaches them.

Conclusion

The world of ISIS is by far not as simple as we are made to think. They are not a terrorist group who hides away from the world and commit suicide bombings. They are far worse. They have the courage, the resources, and the people to act in open field. Even more, they are driven not only by political reasons, but also by a very strong motivation: the desire to enter Paradise.

Civilians living in the areas controlled by ISIS are on edge every single day. Even if most of them welcomed the organization in the beginning, the Islamic state proved to be neither fair nor naive. They are doing everything in their power to control their newly installed Islamic Caliphate; and until now, there seems to be no way of stopping them.